LESSONS
OF THE LAW

A CASEBOOK OF
RACIAL DISCRIMINATION
IN EDUCATION

Cover photograph: Corry Bevington/PHOTOFUSION

First published 1991
ISBN 1 85442 066 6
Price: £3.50

Printed by J.E.C. Potter & Son Ltd., Stamford.

CONTENTS

INTRODUCTION

This booklet presents a collection of cases of racial discrimination in education dealt with by the Commission for Racial Equality (CRE). All the examples are drawn from court or industrial tribunal decisions, from the findings of formal investigations conducted by the Commission under the Race Relations Act 1976, or from advice work with individual clients. The booklet should be read in conjunction with the Commission's *Code of Practice for the Elimination of Racial Discrimination in Education* (1990), which sets out the legal framework on unlawful discrimination and identifies instances where it may occur in all areas of educational provision.

Looking at actual cases will help bring the law and the *Code of Practice* to life. It will:

● Illustrate the human stories underlying legal proceedings.

● Explain the complexities and workings of the law on discrimination in educational contexts.

● Show that legal redress against acts of discrimination in education is possible.

It is important to remember, however, that relatively few cases of discrimination in education have been the subject of legal action, and that the education sections of the Race Relations Act remain relatively untested (compared, for instance, with the employment provisions of the Act). This is understandable, given the nature of county court proceedings, and the difficulty in establishing often complex patterns of discrimination. Nonetheless, the persuasive power of the law to back up advice and information has over the years produced a body of casework which adequately illustrates the impact of the Race Relations Act.

THE LAW

The main provisions of the Race Relations Act 1976 relating to education are set out below, with the number of the appropriate section of the Act in the margin.

The Race Relations Act makes it unlawful to discriminate against someone, directly or indirectly, in the field of education.

S.1(1)(a) Direct discrimination consists of treating a person less favourably than others on racial grounds.

S.1(2) Segregating a person from others on racial grounds is defined as a form of direct discrimination.

S.1(1)(b) Indirect discrimination occurs when:

- a condition or requirement is applied to everyone, but is such that a smaller proportion of a particular racial group can comply with it than others;

- it constitutes a detriment to those who cannot comply;

- it cannot be justified.

S.3 Racial grounds are grounds of race, colour, nationality – including citizenship – or ethnic or national origins, and groups defined by reference to these grounds are referred to as racial groups. A more precise definition of racial group, based on ethnic origins, has been given by the House of Lords. They said that:

- a long shared history; and

- a cultural tradition of its own

were essential characteristics, but that other characteristics were also relevant:

- a common geographical origin, or descent from a small number of common ancestors;

- a common language;

- a common literature;

- a common religion;

- being either a minority or a majority within a larger community.

For the purposes of the Race Relations Act gypsies are defined as a racial group.

S.17   All educational establishments are covered by the Act, and they may not discriminate:

- in the terms on which they offer admission;

- in refusing to accept an application;

- in the way pupils and students are afforded access to any benefits, facilities or services;

- by excluding them from the establishment or subjecting them to any other detriment.

S.18 & 20   It is unlawful for a Local Education Authority (LEA) to discriminate in any form of educational and ancillary provision not already covered by S.17.

S.30 & 31   It is unlawful to instruct or put pressure on others to discriminate.

S.4 It is unlawful for a school, college or LEA to discriminate in employment. This includes recruitment, promotion, conditions of service, dismissal, transfer, training and access to facilities or services provided by the employer. It also covers discrimination in the 'arrangements' made for recruitment and in the way access is provided to opportunities for promotion, transfer or training*.

S.32 An employer is liable for any discriminatory acts done by an employee, unless the employer has taken reasonable steps to prevent such discrimination.

S.71 Local authorities have a general statutory duty to ensure that their various functions are carried out with due regard to the need to:

● eliminate unlawful racial discrimination; and

● promote equality of opportunity and good relations between persons of different racial groups.

*For further details of all aspects of discrimination in employment, see the CRE's *Race Relations Code of Practice: For the elimination of racial discrimination and the promotion of equal opportunity in employment,* 1984.

LAW ENFORCEMENT

The Act provides two forms of legal redress against acts of discrimination: individual complaints and formal investigations conducted by the Commission.

Complaints

Anyone who believes that he or she has suffered discrimination can file a complaint in an industrial tribunal (in employment cases) or initiate proceedings in a county or Sheriff court (in education and other non-employment cases).

In fact, very few education cases have so far been brought to county court (compared to industrial tribunal employment cases). This is probably because:

- The cases will involve parents and children who may be in some distress about their treatment and reluctant to take matters to a court.

- Sympathetic schools and LEAs may seek an amicable out of court settlement.

- All non-employment complaints against public sector education bodies must first be referred to the Secretary of State for Education, who has two months in which to look into the matter before it can be taken further. Legal procedures are such that a lapse of up to three years can occur between an allegation of discrimination and its judicial resolution, thus deterring potential complainants.

Complainants may apply to the Commission for assistance in both employment and non-employment cases. This may include:

- Advice

- Procuring a settlement

- Legal representation

Investigations

The Commission has the power under the Race Relations Act to conduct formal investigations into suspected discrimination by schools, colleges and LEAs. If the proposed investigation is into a named institution, the Commission must:

- Have grounds for belief that discrimination may have occurred.

- Issue terms of reference for the investigation.

- Offer the named institution an opportunity to make representations concerning the proposed investigation.

If an investigation reaches a finding of unlawful discrimination, the Commission may issue a non-discrimination notice, except in cases of public sector education bodies where the Secretary of State has enforcement powers.

Proceedings brought by the Commission

In the case of alleged breaches of S.29, 30 and 31 (discriminatory advertisements, instructions and pressure to discriminate), proceedings can only be brought by the Commission for Racial Equality in a county or Sheriff court.

ADMISSIONS, EXCLUSIONS AND TRANSFERS

A number of cases concerning admissions, exclusions and transfers have involved rules about uniform and appearance.

Mandla v Dowell Lee

In 1978, Mr Sewa Singh Mandla, a Sikh, tried to enrol his son as a pupil at a private school in Birmingham. The headteacher of the school, Mr Dowell Lee, refused to admit the boy to the school unless he complied with the school's uniform rules by removing his turban and cutting his hair.

With the Commission's assistance, Mr Mandla took the case to Birmingham County Court, where he argued that the headteacher's 'no turban' rule constituted unlawful indirect discrimination under S.1(1)(b) of the Race Relations Act, because:

- The school's uniform rule constituted a test, condition or requirement which his son could not comply with because of the cultural norms of Sikhs as a racial group.

- The rule could not be justified.

The County Court dismissed Mr Mandla's claim, and held that:

- His son could physically comply with the requirement by removing his turban.

- The 'no turban' ban was justifiable in terms of the purposes of the uniform rules.

- Sikhs were not a racial group as defined by the Race Relations Act 1976.

After an unsuccessful appeal in the Court of Appeal, the Mandlas, again with the Commission's assistance, took the case to the House of Lords in 1983, where the appeal was upheld. The Lords ruled that:

- The term, 'can comply', in the Act should not be interpreted in a literal, physical sense, but construed as meaning 'can in practice comply', consistent with the customs and cultural norms of the racial group.

- The 'no turbans' rule could not be justified on educational grounds.

- Sikhs were an ethnic group under the Race Relations Act.

The *Mandla* case is significant, not just from a legal perspective, but also in terms of its application to school admissions criteria. The Lords' liberal interpretation of 'can comply' in terms of cultural practices means that conditions or requirements which have a disproportionate effect for cultural reasons may be covered by the legal concept of indirect discrimination.

In the particular context of school admissions criteria and policies, this means that uniform and dress regulations which result in the rejection of a pupil who cannot comply with them for cultural or religious reasons are likely to be unlawful.

The *Mandla* case is also important in the more general context of the legal definition of an 'ethnic group'. The House of Lords judgment set out a more explicit checklist of defining factors than the Act's definition of a 'racial group' (see pp 6-7). Two essential characteristics of an ethnic group were described as:

- A long shared history.

- A common cultural tradition of its own.

But other characteristics were also deemed relevant:

- A common geographical origin, or descent from a small number of common ancestors.

- A common language.

- A common literature.

- A common religion.

- Being either a minority or a majority within a larger community.

A subsequent case led to the inclusion of gypsies as a racial group.

Girls and uniform requirements

The most recent, and much publicised, case of Muslim girls alleging discrimination over school uniform arose when the Alvi sisters from Altrincham made the news in their fight to wear *hijab* (headscarf/veil). The Commission supported the girls' view that to deny them the right to wear a garment for religious reasons constituted indirect racial discrimination, given that such a rule would disproportionately affect people from the Asian subcontinent. The school and the LEA accepted this advice.

The case had several precedents, all of which had been resolved in different ways:

- In 1987, a headteacher excluded two Muslim sisters from school in an outer London borough when they wanted to wear *shalwar kameez* (trouser suit) in school colours, for religious reasons. Despite the LEA's equal opportunity policy, the headteacher's decision was supported by the school's governing body.

  The Commission was in regular contact with the Chief Education Officer, who, on his own initiative, put the matter before the Education Committee. Despite warnings of possible unlawful racial discrimination, the Committee upheld the decision.

The Commission, the local Racial Equality Council (REC), community groups and the parents continued to press for a lawful resolution of the impasse, which had kept the girls out of school for a whole term. In the event, a meeting of the full Council resolved that it was an act of unlawful racial discrimination to deny the girls their wishes in respect of the uniform, and affirmed that this would not happen again.

● A similar case hit the headlines about a girls' school in a small rural town, with a equal opportunity policy. But here the head-teacher claimed that she had consulted Muslim organisations before deciding to exclude the two girls who wanted to wear *shalwar kameez* in school colours, again for conscientiously-held religious reasons. The school claimed that it was already catering for such religious views by allowing Muslim girls to wear ankle-length skirts.

The Commission also consulted a range of Muslim organisa-tions and explained to the school that modesty in dress was observed in different ways by different ethnic groups, and that this needed to be respected. Here, again, the governors supported the headteacher, although they were advised that to exclude the girls for refusing to wear the correct, permitted school uniform was likely to be unlawful.

The Commission finally succeeded in persuading the school to agree to the girls' request, and the uniform regulations were amended. However, in this case too, the girls missed many weeks of schooling.

St George's Hospital Medical School

In 1987, the Commission conducted a formal investigation into St George's Hospital Medical School (University of London) following allegations of racial discrimination in the admission of students to the undergraduate MB,BS degree course. The Commission found that St

George's had directly discriminated on racial grounds by using a computer program to sort application forms which gave adverse weightings to ethnic minority candidates, thereby reducing their chances of admission.

The discrimination at St George's was discovered by chance when Dr Joe Collier, a lecturer at the school, watched the admissions officer processing application forms at a computer. Dr Collier noticed the questions:

Male: Yes or No?

Caucasian: Yes or No?

As an experiment, he and the officer entered a student first as a male Caucasian, and then as a female non-Caucasian*. The computer ranking for the same student as a 'male Caucasian' was 19, and as a 'female non-Caucasian', 37. The lower the score, the better the ranking (see page 16). It was common knowledge at the school that the rankings were used as the basis for deciding whether a student would be called for interview, and it became clear immediately that the program discriminated against women and ethnic minority candidates.

In common with many other universities and colleges, the admissions procedure at St George's consisted of three stages:

- Selection for interview.

- Interview.

- Admission through 'clearing'.

About 25 per cent of all applicants were selected for interview, about 70 per cent of those interviewed were offered places, and only a minority were finally admitted at the clearing stage.

In 1973, Dr Franglen, one of the selectors, began work on a computer program to evaluate the application forms. He took into account not only academic performance, but all the other relevant

---

*Caucasian and non-Caucasian were the terms used by the School to define ethnic origin.

selection criteria as well. Dr Franglen did this by observing the decisions of selectors over a number of years and adjusting the program accordingly; his aim was to *mimic* the selectors' judgements.

By 1979, Dr Franglen had achieved a 90-95 per cent correlation with the gradings of the selection panel, and the program was introduced to run alongside selectors' examination of the UCCA (Universities Central Council on Admissions) forms. From 1982, all selection for interview was done by the computer alone.

The program operated by assigning a percentile ranking to each applicant, based on a scoring of the various factors in the application form: the lower the score, the better the ranking. In any one year only those within a certain range of top rankings were called for interview.

The program assessed two sorts of factors: academic and personal. Academic factors included 'O' and 'A' levels (number, grade, subjects), and accounted for 75 per cent of the final score. Personal factors included the headteacher's report, age, sports and hobbies, social and community work, handwriting, type of school, etc - and race and sex.

Ethnic minority and female applicants were both given negative weightings: for female candidates, the personal score was multiplied by 1.05, for ethnic minority males by 1.33, and for ethnic minority females by 1.3965. This increased the applicants' computer scores, and correspondingly lowered their percentile rankings, thus reducing their chances of being called for interview. It was estimated that about 60 ethnic minority applicants per year were thus denied the opportunity of an interview and were discriminated against.

The investigation also considered the possibility of discrimination at the interview stage itself. It was found that 57 per cent of ethnic minority interviewees were offered places, compared with 72 per cent of white interviewees. Although these discrepancies were statistically significant, only one year's figures were available, and it was decided to keep this part of the investigation open, pending annual reports on the monitoring of applications and admissions by the school for the next three years.

Finally, the investigation found that a far higher proportion of ethnic minority students than white students were being admitted through 'clearing' (at the end of the admissions cycle) – 37 per cent compared with 13 per cent, respectively, in 1986. This was not because of any 'reverse' discrimination in favour of ethnic minority applicants, but probably because the discrimination earlier on in the selection process had excluded a disproportionately large number of well-qualified ethnic minority applicants, so that there were more of them to be considered at the clearing stage than white applicants.

The St George's case raises a number of important issues, not only in terms of medical school admissions but also more generally regarding discrimination and equality of opportunity in higher education.

- First, the investigation showed that discrimination can occur where it is least expected. St George's is a liberal, forward-looking university institution whose charter and ethos proscribe any form of discrimination, and which has an above average number of ethnic minority students (19 per cent in 1986). Indeed, the relatively large number of ethnic minority students lulled the school into a false sense of complacency that it could not possibly be discriminating against them. Colleges intending to monitor equality of opportunity in admissions will therefore need to compare applications with intake and not simply rely on enrolment data.

- Second, the St George's investigation also raises the issue of responsibility in educational institutions. Under S.32 of the Race Relations Act, an employer is liable for the actions of his or her employees, unless reasonable steps have been taken to ensure that they do not discriminate. By not checking on the selection criteria in the computer program, the school authorities manifestly failed to take such steps.

- Finally, the case of St George's shows that discrimination can be identified and measured. The fact that the computer program was able to replicate so accurately the decisions made by selectors means that any bias in the admissions criteria can be quantified and eliminated.

During the course of the investigation and subsequently, the school has taken concrete steps to monitor admissions and eliminate discrimination

Cleveland LEA

In November 1987, Cleveland LEA received a letter from the parent of a primary school pupil requesting that her daughter be transferred to another school. Her reason was:

> I don't think it's fair for (her) to go through school with about four white friends and the rest Pakistan (sic), which she does not associate with. I think the school is very good, but I don't think it's right when she comes home singing in Pakistan. I know they only learn three Pakistan songs but I don't want her to learn this language.... I just want her to go to a school where there will be a majority of white children not Pakistani.

The racial composition of the school the child was attending was 40 per cent Asian and 60 per cent white; the school to which her mother was requesting a transfer was 98 per cent white.

The LEA and the headteachers of both schools tried to persuade the parent that there was no sound reason for the transfer, that it might not be in the best educational interests of her child, and that the curriculum provided in the two schools was substantially the same. The parent did not accept this advice, and the transfer took place.

In its investigation of this incident, the Commission's primary concern was to establish whether or not the LEA's compliance with a parental preference based on racial grounds constituted a breach of the Race Relations Act 1976. Cleveland LEA was itself reluctant to accede to the parent's request, believing it to be founded on racial prejudice, but felt that it was obliged to do so, under education law.

Under S.6 of the Education Act 1980, an LEA is required to make arrangements to enable parents to express a preference as to the school they want their child to attend. The LEA also has a duty to comply with such a preference, unless, by agreeing to do so it would prejudice the LEA's provision of efficient education or the efficient use of resources; for example, if the school is already full.

In Cleveland LEA's view, the fact that the parent's preference was based on racial grounds and would result in an act of discrimination did not absolve it from its duty to comply with that preference.

The Commission took the opposite view and contended that, under S.18 of the Race Relations Act, an LEA could not carry out any of its functions (including transfers) if they involved acts of unlawful discrimination - in this case, segregation. The Commission believed that Cleveland LEA was in breach of the Race Relations Act by complying with the preference.

In essence, then, the investigation amounted to a dispute over LEA obligations under different pieces of legislation. Should an LEA always comply with a parental preference (S.6 of the Education Act 1980) or should it refuse to do so if compliance led to unlawful discrimination (S.18 of the Race Relations Act)?

In the case of public sector education bodies (including LEAs), the Commission does not have the power to issue a non-discrimination notice, but can only refer its findings to the Secretary of State, asking him or her to tell LEAs that they must not comply with parental preferences made on racial grounds. Apart from the legal question of whether or not the Race Relations Act 1976 overrides the Education Act 1980, the Cleveland case raises the important issue of the extent to which racial considerations influence parents' choices of schools, and the possible consequences if they do.

If significant numbers of parents did select schools because of their racial composition, and opted for 'same-race' schools, the result would be a degree of racial segregation between schools. The Commission drew this to the Government's attention during the passage of the Education Reform Bill in 1987, and remains concerned that the open enrolment provisions of the Education Reform Act

1988 may exacerbate the situation.

In the Cleveland case, the Secretary of State rejected the Commission's finding of unlawful discrimination. The Commission decided to apply to the High Court for a judicial review of the Secretary of State's decision, in order to establish the principle at the heart of this case. At the time of writing, we are awaiting a date for the hearing.

SUSPENSIONS

Birmingham LEA

In 1979, the Commission decided to conduct a formal investigation into school suspensions, an issue which had caused widespread concern for many years. Birmingham LEA was selected as the site of the investigation, not because the Commission had any reason to believe that it was unique in this respect, but rather because it was a representative example of a large, urban, multi-racial education authority.

In the early 1970s, Birmingham was one of the first LEAs to recognise the growing problem of pupils being suspended from school. To deal with it, the LEA set up two educational guidance centres for pupils with behavioural problems and three special units for suspended pupils. The focus of the Commission's investigation was the procedures and criteria used by Birmingham schools between 1974-80 to suspend pupils and refer them to special units.

The investigation showed that:

- Ethnic minority pupils were four times more likely to be suspended than white pupils for similar offences.

- Ethnic minority pupils were three times more likely to be placed in suspension units than white pupils.

- Ethnic minority pupils were six times more likely to be suspended under the age of 14 than white pupils.

- 43 per cent of the pupils in the special units were of Afro-Caribbean origin, whereas only 10 per cent of Birmingham's school population were from this racial group.

- Ethnic minority pupils were more likely to be suspended or referred after shorter periods of 'disruptive' behaviour than white pupils.

Birmingham LEA's explanation for these disparities was that ethnic minority pupils were overrepresented in inner city schools and among children from a one parent family background.

In other words, the LEA was claiming that the disparities in suspension or referral rates were not caused by race as such, but by other social factors.

The Commission's statistical analyses demonstrated, however, that the inner city factor only accounted for a small amount of ethnic minority overrepresentation among suspended pupils, and that the single parent factor appeared to have a more aggravating effect on white rather than ethnic minority pupils. The Commission concluded, therefore, that the race factor was significant in the differential suspension and referral rates.

SEPARATE PROVISION (ESL)

Calderdale LEA

Calderdale is an LEA in West Yorkshire centred on the town of Halifax. According to the 1981 census, it had an ethnic minority population of 3.4 per cent, the majority of whom were Pakistanis from Mirpur.

The cause for concern in Calderdale, which became the subject of a formal investigation by the Commission in 1985, was the arrangements made by the LEA for the teaching of English as a second language. The LEA's arrangements were that:

- All children newly arrived or recently returned from the Indian subcontinent, and all those born in the UK whose first language was not English, had to take a language test, to determine whether they required special ESL tuition.

- Children who did not pass the language test were placed in a separate language class or language centre.

The arrangements had several effects:

- Nearly all the children taking the language test were of Asian origin.

- Up to 80 per cent of the Asian children in Calderdale schools had spent some time - between 1 and 2.5 years - in a language unit.

- Half the language units were situated outside the areas of Asian settlement, which meant that some of the children were 'bussed'. These children, compared to those attending their local school, spent more time travelling, and could lose part of the school day.

- The curriculum followed in the language units was often narrower than in mainstream schools, and, at secondary level, did not have specialist subject teachers.

- The parents of children in language units could not appeal against their child's placement, had no opportunity to express a school preference, and, in some cases, could not take part in elections to governing bodies.

Calderdale LEA contended that its policy of placing ESL pupils in separate units and excluding them from mainstream schooling was justifiable, because it had been introduced at a time when language withdrawal was considered to be educationally sound.

On the basis of current theory and research on second language acquisition, the Commission came to the conclusion that language withdrawal methods involving separate provision could not be justified on educational grounds. Increasingly, linguists were of the view that the best ESL learning and teaching environment was one in which language is used within the mainstream classroom and curriculum, and that withdrawal is counterproductive.

The Commission's investigation therefore concluded that Calderdale's ESL arrangements constituted unlawful indirect discrimination in that:

- The language test amounted to a condition or requirement.

- The proportion of Asian pupils who could comply with it was smaller than other racial groups.

- Separate language unit placement meant that pupils and parents suffered a detriment.

- The practice could not be shown to be justifiable on educational grounds.

The Commission referred its findings to the Secretary of State for Education, who agreed that Calderdale's provision was unlawful and instructed the LEA to introduce new arrangements for ESL – which it has now done.

The Calderdale case is important for two main reasons.

- First, it establishes that separate provision, where it involves exclusion from mainstream schooling and cannot be justified on educational grounds, is unlawful.

- Second, it highlights how educational practices and procedures can have a discriminatory effect regardless of their intentions. There is no doubt that Calderdale LEA and the teachers working in the language services were doing what they thought was in the best interests of the children. It was only on closer inspection that it became clear that the apparent benefits of the language units were outweighed by their adverse consequences.

In this respect, Calderdale represents a 'textbook' example of indirect discrimination; the resulting inequalities originated from the operation of the system rather than from the intentions or motives of individuals.

DRESS

Rasta dreadlocks

A 14 year-old boy who decided to adopt the Rastafarian faith found himself facing discrimination at his coeducational school in an outer London borough. The school had no specific policy or guidelines for dealing with questions of hairstyle and dress related to religious beliefs.

The boy adopted the Rastafarian faith during the summer and started to grow his hair into 'locks'. He and his mother were asked to ensure that his hair was 'properly' cut. The boy, supported by his mother, stood by his faith. The mother contacted the Commission over what she saw as the harassment of her child by some of the teachers at the school.

The Commission contacted the local REC, which succeeded in making the school understand that since a ban on the Rastafarian hairstyle would have a disproportionate effect on a particular ethnic group, this could constitute unlawful racial discrimination, for which the school would be liable in law.

Sikh bangles

The Deputy Head of a coeducational comprehensive contacted the Commission to discuss the question of prohibiting Sikh sixth-formers from wearing the Sikh bangle because 'It might cause injury to themselves or to others, particularly in games or physical education classes'.

The Commission explained to the school that this was likely to be unlawful, because of the requirements of the Sikh religion. The school came up with a novel, if not entirely satisfactory, solution; in future, Sikh bangles might be worn so long as they were out of sight under a boy's shirt sleeve.

WORK EXPERIENCE

CRE v Fearn and British Electrical Repairs (BER)

In January 1986, a teacher at Selhurst High School in Croydon telephoned Mr David Fearn, the manager of a local electrical repair firm, BER, to discuss the possibility of work experience placements for two Selhurst pupils. The teacher was responsible for organising placements for the Certificate in Pre-Vocational Education (CPVE), which involves an element of work experience with local employers. The teacher had no prior knowledge of BER or Mr Fearn, and had simply selected the firm from the phone book. He explained the nature and purpose of work experience and the CPVE, and Mr Fearn invited him to visit the factory the next day.

After an extensive tour of the factory the following afternoon, the teacher discussed the details of the work experience placement with Mr Fearn. The boys in question were described as two well-motivated and pleasant young 'West Indian' boys.

There was a moment's awkwardness. The teacher asked if the boys' racial origin was a problem, to which Mr Fearn replied that, as far as he was concerned, it was not. However, he did not think his workforce would accept it, and that it would not be a good idea to proceed with the placement. Mr Fearn then fumbled for further, non-racial reasons to exclude the two boys, such as educational attainment and maturity.

Giving evidence later, the teacher also alleged that Mr Fearn had suggested that perhaps the firm could start with two other boys first, and that if that was a success he could take the two West Indian lads on another occasion.

The teacher was shocked and upset, and decided that no Selhurst pupils could be placed at BER. He reported the incident to his colleagues at the school the next day. The headteacher wrote to Croydon's Chief Education Officer, who referred the matter to the Commission.

When the case came to Westminster County Court, the judge ruled that Mr Fearn had been in breach of S.31 of the Race Relations Act, in that he had attempted to induce the teacher to discriminate against the two boys by not sending them to the factory. The judge also concluded that BER was in breach of S.32 of the Race Relations Act, in that the firm was liable for the actions of its employees and had not taken sufficient steps to ensure that they did not discriminate.

The Croydon case is important for a number of reasons:

- Work experience placements form an increasingly significant element in secondary and further education, and afford ample opportunity for employers to exert pressure on schools to discriminate.

- If the teacher had complied with the request and sent two white boys, the school would have been in breach of S.17 of the Race Relations Act by not affording the two ethnic minority pupils access to educational facilities on racial grounds.

- It was only because of prompt action by the teacher, in the context of the school's equal opportunities policy, that the matter came to light.

- Although BER had an equal opportunity policy, it did not absolve the firm of liability under S.32; the policy was not being monitored, nor had staff been trained in its implications and implementation.

CHARGING POLICIES

Travel costs

An outer London borough's decision to withdraw payments for travel costs outside the borough has had a disproportionate effect on Jewish pupils. While Roman Catholic and Church of England pupils are similarly affected, there are nevertheless schools that can meet their religious needs within the borough boundaries; no such schools exist for Jewish children.

Despite a protracted exchange of correspondence with the Commission, the matter has not still been resolved. The LEA refuses to accept that this may be indirectly discriminatory on racial grounds. It is possible that cases will be brought against the authority by two individual complainants, and the matter resolved in the county court.

Differential charges

In 1989, the Commission intervened when a local Community Relations Council (now Racial Equality Council) drew attention to a case of possibly unlawful discrimination: the Adult Education Institute was charging a fee of £50.00 per course for adult ESL classes, but not for adult literacy classes.

The Principal of the Adult Education Institute was advised by the adult literacy organiser, Her Majesty's Inspectorate, and the local community relations officer that this might be unlawful under the Race Relations Act, as the literacy classes were more likely to be attended by English people, while the ESL classes would undoubtedly cater predominantly for members of ethnic minority groups.

The Institute agreed, in the circumstances, to withdraw the differential charges, but did not acknowledge that it had been guilty of unlawful racial discrimination.

EXAMINATION BODIES

The Commission was approached by a Chief Education Officer who was concerned about a Vietnamese boy about to take his chemistry GCSE examination. In accordance with the examination body's regulations, he was allowed to take a bilingual dictionary into the exam, but he was not allowed any extra time to do the exam. By contrast, other categories of pupils with particular educational needs were allowed an extra 25 per cent of time for the exam.

The examination board said that it was acting under the rules of a wider joint body, and that it was not at liberty to depart from them. The Head of the joint body advised the local examination board that it could, and should, use its discretion to allow the Vietnamese boy extra time, and undertook to review the rule altogether.

EMPLOYMENT

Singh v London Borough of Newham (Director of Education)

Mr Singh was a teacher at Stratford School in East London, appointed under S.11 of the Local Government Act 1966*.

In February 1987, the LEA wrote to all secondary school head teachers advising them that teachers appointed under S.11 should not be considered for any internal promotions. In the LEA's view, S.11 teachers were not ordinary members of staff but only 'attached' to particular schools.

As a result, Mr Singh was specifically excluded from applying for the post of Head of Third Year at Stratford School, because the LEA decided that the post should only be advertised internally (that is, within the school).

At the London (North) Industrial Tribunal in 1988, Mr Singh, represented by the National Union of Teachers, argued that the LEA's refusal to consider his (or any other S.11 teacher's) application constituted indirect discrimination in the arrangements made for promotions.

Mr Singh argued that:

- The exclusion of S.11 teachers from consideration for promotion constituted a condition or requirement, in this case the negative requirement that they should not be S.11 teachers.

- The proportion of ethnic minority teachers who could comply with the requirement was smaller than others, because ethnic minority teachers in Newham were disproportionately employed under S.11.

*Section 11 allows the Home Office to provide grants to local authorities to appoint staff to meet the special needs of pupils of Commonwealth origin.

- The requirement could not be justified.

The LEA conceded that the restriction of applications to internal, non-S.11 staff could have an adverse effect on particular racial groups, and weaken its equal opportunities policy. However, it argued that this was justifiable, because:

- S.11 teachers were in 'above ratio' posts attached to schools, and were primarily based in the multi-racial support services.

- The promotion of an 'external' S.11 teacher would lead to difficulties over Home Office funding.

- Financial considerations and budgetary restrictions forced the LEA to consider only 'internal' applicants.

The tribunal rejected these arguments and found that the LEA had indirectly discriminated against Mr Singh. The tribunal also declared that, although Mr Singh was a S.11 teacher, he should have been regarded as a permanent member of staff at Stratford School.

There are three important aspects to this case:

- It shows that discrimination can occur even where the employer has an explicit equal opportunities policy and is committed to the elimination of discrimination.

- It also demonstrates that discrimination can occur not only at the point of recruitment/promotion but also in the arrangements made and in the procedures followed to determine eligibility for promotion.

- It raises the issue of the employment status of S.11 teachers. Although the tribunal defined them as members of staff at the schools where they were placed, the picture may now be more complicated by the employment and financial delegation provisions of the Education Reform Act 1988 and new Home Office criteria for S.11 funding (Circular 78/1990).

Arora v Bradford Metropolitan Council

In April 1987, Ms Ranjit Arora, Head of Multicultural Education at Bradford and Ilkely College since 1983, applied for the post of Head of Teaching Studies at the same college. Three candidates were shortlisted for interview: Ms Arora, Mr Hassall (then acting Head of Teaching Studies) and Miss Montford, an external applicant. Ms Arora was the only ethnic minority candidate.

The selection procedure at the college involved two interviews: the first was a 'biographical' interview in the morning, to decide which (if any) of the candidates were to proceed to the second, formal interview in the afternoon. Mr Hassall was the only candidate selected for a second interview, and was duly appointed.

In December, Ms Arora brought a case, assisted by the Commission, to the industrial tribunal, alleging discrimination under both the Race Relations Act and the Sex Discrimination Act. The essence of her complaint was that, because of discrimination in the first interview, she was not given the chance to proceed to the second, formal interview.

The purpose of the 'biographical' interview was to give candidates the opportunity to expand on their history, qualifications and experience, and to 'sell' themselves to the selection committee.

The tribunal came to the view that the panel, chaired by Dr Gallagher, the college principal, conducted the interview in such a way as to prejudice Ms Arora's chances. In particular, it found that:

● Undue emphasis was placed on her cultural and ethnic background.

● No account was taken of her extensive research experience.

● Too little attention was paid to her managerial experience.

This last point was crucial. The selection panel regarded managerial experience as the most important qualification. They were keen to appoint someone with sufficient 'clout', who would be able to negotiate with the outside bodies responsible for the organisation and validation of teacher education. Ms Arora was simply not given the opportunity to demonstrate these vital qualities. As the tribunal said:

> ... this applicant was not taken through this interview in a full and proper, non-discriminatory way, because the arrangements at the interview directly denied her the opportunities to show her abilities fairly.

The tribunal did not question the outstanding qualities of the successful candidate, Mr Hassall; the issue was that Ms Arora had not been given the opportunity to highlight her qualifications and experience. In these circumstances, Mr Hassall's eventual appointment was, as the tribunal put it, a 'self fulfilling prophecy'.

The Tribunal awarded Ms Arora £500 as compensation for injury to feelings and costs against the Council. Following further legal proceedings, the Court of Appeal awarded exemplary damages of £2000 against Bradford Council.

The most important aspects of this case are that:

● The discrimination did not lie in the fact that Ms Arora was not appointed, but in the fact that the way she was questioned in the first interview prevented her from moving on to the next stage of the selection process to be considered formally.

● It demonstrates that discrimination can occur even where the college and the LEA have a high profile commitment to, and explicit policy on, equal opportunities.

● It shows that public bodies (such as local authorities and their institutions) may be liable for exemplary damages if they are found to have acted in breach of the Race Relations Act.

CONCLUSIONS

The cases described in this booklet illustrate the various forms, and the complexity, of racial discrimination in education. Given the small number of cases that have been the subject of legal proceedings, one may be forgiven for thinking that this indicates its relative rarity. Surely, one might argue, the professional dedication, beliefs and values of those in the education service are such that acts of discrimination will be the exception rather than the rule?

The Commission would not wish to question the commitment of teachers, lecturers and administrators to treat all pupils, students and colleagues in a fair and equal way regardless of race. Indeed, many LEAs and institutions now have equal opportunity statements to this effect.

However, as most of the examples in this booklet indicate, discrimination is rarely overt or motivated by malice. More often it is unconscious, unintended or the result of applying requirements that have an indirectly discriminatory effect. Consequently, discrimination in education may be *more* rather than less extensive than the cases in this booklet at first suggest.

Moreover, most existing race equality policies in education have little to say about discrimination and the law as such. They tend to concentrate on the questions of ethnic diversity, prejudice and the role of education in promoting a multicultural ethos. However important these issues are, and the policies and practices they have generated, they are not helpful in addressing the issue of equal treatment before the law.

Whatever its limitations, the Race Relations Act does precisely this, and redirects the focus of educational provision to the problems of access and opportunity. It was for this purpose that the Commission produced its *Code of Practice for the Elimination of Racial*

Discrimination in Education. This casebook is intended to complement the Code by providing examples of how discrimination has occurred in education. We hope, too, that both this booklet and the Code will be used widely for equal opportunity training and policy development in schools, colleges and LEAs.

COMMISSION FOR RACIAL EQUALITY

The Commission for Racial Equality was set up by the Race Relations
Act 1976 with the duties of:

- Working towards the elimination of discrimination.

- Promoting equality of opportunity and good relations between
  persons of different racial groups.

- Keeping under review the working of the Act, and, when required
  by the Secretary of State or when it otherwise thinks it is necessary,
  drawing up and submitting to the Secretary of State proposals for
  amending it.

London (Head Office)

Elliot House
10-12 Allington Street
London SW1E 5EH
☎ 071-828 7022
FAX 071-630 7605

Birmingham

Alpha Tower (11th floor)
Suffolk Street Queensway
Birmingham B1 1TT
☎ 021-632 4544
FAX 021-643 3492

Leeds

Yorkshire Bank Chambers
(1st floor)
Infirmary Street
Leeds LS1 2JP
☎ 0532-434413
FAX 0532-443213

Manchester

Maybrook House (5th floor)
40 Blackfriars Street
Manchester M3 2EG
☎ 061-831 7782
FAX 061-833 2186

Leicester

Haymarket House (4th floor)
Haymarket Shopping Centre
Leicester LE1 3YG
☎ 0533-517852
FAX 0533-515359

Scotland

100 Princes Street
Edinburgh EH2 3AA
☎ 031-226 5186
FAX 031-266 5343